Children of the World

Brazil

For their help in the preparation of *Children of the World: Brazil*, the editors gratefully thank Employment and Immigration Canada, Ottawa, Ont.; the US Immigration and Naturalization Service, Washington, DC; the Embassy of Brazil (US), Washington, DC; the International Institute of Wisconsin, Milwaukee; the United States Department of State, Bureau of Public Affairs, Office of Public Communication, Washington, DC, for unencumbered use of material in the public domain; and Tricia Cornell Barreto.

Library of Congress Cataloging-in-Publication Data

Ikuhara, Yoshiyuki, 1947-
    Brazil.

    (Children of the world)
    Bibliography: p.
    Includes index.
    Summary: Presents the life of Andre and Camille who live with their parents outside of Rio de Janeiro, Brazil, describing their home and school activities and the festivals, religious ceremonies, and national holidays of their countries.
    1. Brazil—Social life and custom—Juvenile literature. 2. Children—Brazil—Juvenile literature. [1. Family life—Brazil. 2. Brazil—Social life and customs] I. Sherwood, Rhoda. II. Title. III. Series: Children of the world (Milwaukee, Wis.)
F2510.I49 1988   981'.063   87-42579
ISBN 1-55532-246-8
ISBN 1-55532-221-2 (lib. bdg.)

North American edition first published in 1988 by
Gareth Stevens, Inc.
7317 West Green Tree Road Milwaukee, Wisconsin 53223, USA

This work was originally published in shortened form consisting of section I only. Photographs and original text copyright © 1987 by Yoshiyuki Ikuhara. First and originally published by Kaisei-sha Publishing Co., Ltd., Tokyo. World English rights arranged with Kaisei-sha Publishing Co., Ltd. through Japan Foreign-Rights Centre.

Typeset by Ries Graphics ltd., Milwaukee.
Design: Laurie Bishop and Laurie Shock.
Map design: Kate Kriege.

3 4 5 6 7 8 9 92 91 90 89

Printed in the United States of America

Children of the World

Brazil

Photography by
Yoshiyuki Ikuhara

Edited
by
Rhoda Sherwood

Gareth Stevens Publishing
Milwaukee

. . . a note about *Children of the World:*

The children of the world live in fishing towns, Arctic regions, and urban centers, on islands and in mountain valleys, on sheep ranches and fruit farms. This series follows one child in each country through the pattern of his or her life. Candid photographs show the children with their families, at school, at play, and in their communities. The text describes the dreams of the children and, often through their own words, tells how they see themselves and their lives.

Each book also explores events that are unique to the country in which the child lives, including festivals, religious ceremonies, and national holidays. The *Children of the World* series does more than tell about foreign countries. It introduces the children of each country and shows readers what it is like to be a child in that country.

. . . and about *Brazil:*

André and Camille are from Brazil, a country that occupies almost half of South America. They enjoy both the busy pace of modern Rio de Janeiro and the quiet, traditional quality of Santa Teresa Hill, an old section of downtown Rio where they live with their parents. Rio is one of the largest cities in South America and is world-famous for its carnivals.

To enhance this book's value in libraries and classrooms, comprehensive reference sections include up-to-date data about Brazil's geography, demographics, language, currency, education, culture, industry, and natural resources. *Brazil* also features a bibliography, research topics, activity projects, and discussions of such subjects as Brasília, the country's history, political system, ethnic and religious composition, and language.

The living conditions and experiences of children in Brazil vary tremendously according to economic, environmental, and ethnic circumstances. The reference sections help bring to life for young readers the diversity and richness of the culture and heritage of Brazil. Of particular interest are discussions of Brazil's vast and varied geography and of the many cultures and national groups that have made their presence felt in the nation's language and traditions.

CONTENTS

The Manez-Silver family in front of their home.

LIVING IN BRAZIL:
Camille and André, Two Cariocas

Rio de Janeiro is in Brazil, the fifth largest country in the world. It covers almost half of South America. On Santa Teresa Hill in Rio live Camille and André Manez-Silver and their parents, Marli and Elías. Like all residents of Rio, they are called *Cariocas*.

This family is wealthy, so they can afford a large house in this pleasant part of Rio. Santa Teresa Hill is not like modern Rio, where tourists crowd the seashores. The Hill is old and quiet. The family enjoys living here. André has a view of the city from his bedroom window. Camille watches the birds, squirrels, and monkeys. Nearby is an aqueduct built in 1750 to carry water to the city. The Santa Teresa Hill streetcar climbs up the hill close to the houses.

From left: Elías, Camille, Marli, and André.

Rio de Janeiro with Pão de Açucar (Sugar Loaf Mountain), a familiar symbol of Rio.

Family Living

Both parents work. Elías owns an antique store. Mornings, Marli manages the business import section of a government bank. Tuesday and Thursday afternoons, she counsels at a clinic in Copacabana, a section of Rio.¹ Like many middle-class and wealthy families in Brazil, the Manez-Silvers have maids, but on weekends they like to eat meals together, shop, and share some chores. Camille and André want to go to college in the United States. They have been told most people there have no maids, so they are learning how to take care of themselves.

The family eats little meat but lots of vegetables, beans, rice, and macaroni, which André likes. Marli likes *manjioca*, a kind of potato. There is lots of fruit in Brazil, so they always eat it for dessert and often enjoy it as a snack.

"Do you want something to drink, Camille?"

From the top right: macaroni, rice, olives, limes, manjioca, greens, and, in the middle, *feijão* (beans).

"Are you sure children in the United States do dishes?"

Working together gives them a chance to talk.

Camille, André, and their father like television.

Lunch is the large meal in Brazil, so the family has only a light snack in the evening. Sometimes they just munch on popcorn while they watch television. Marli does not like television that much but she likes being with her family, so sometimes she joins them.

André reads comics on the weekend.

Reading on the living room floor.

This is a bit more comfortable.

Camille and André's parents met when both were students at Gamafillo University. They want their children to go to college too, so they encourage them to read. There are magazines, newspapers, and books in the home.

Many Brazilian children never go to school. Poverty is a problem in this country, so it is common for children to work to help support their families. The government has even asked that businesses set aside a certain number of jobs just for children ages 12 through 18, but not many businesses have done this.

13

"Did you say he was ironing?"

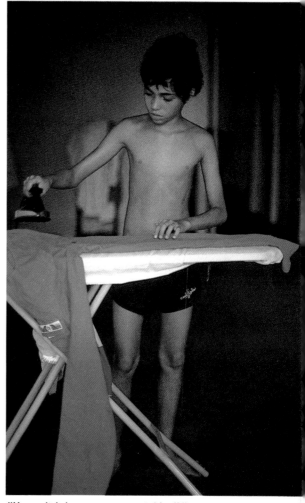

"How did these get so wrinkled?"

Camille and André Are Never Bored!

André, who is 12 years old, wants
to go out and play with his friends.
He likes swimming, video games, and soccer, Brazil's most
popular sport. Maracanã, the largest soccer stadium in the
world, is in Rio, and André often goes there with friends.

André practices ironing today, thinking he may have to do
this in the States. His friends wait near the stone wall. Many
homes in Brazil are surrounded by walls or fences.

14

The dogs were bought to prevent burglaries when no one is home.

"I know the answer to this one."

André and a friend plan a game.

André collects bottle caps.

"I wonder if I should clean this drawer."

Camille, who is 11, wants to be a fashion model or an actress. She has already acted as an extra in a couple of movies, and she is not shy at all about being in front of the camera. She likes to have fun, and she is outgoing around people, so she is popular. Because she goes to school quite far from home, she has two sets of friends, those in school and those in the neighborhood.

"Do actresses wear flowers in their hair?"

Camille and a friend play a video game.

Camille studies at Marli's desk.

Camille has so many interests that she is never bored. Besides acting, she likes drawing and writing. Every day is filled with activities that amuse her.

But Camille also does her homework. Brazilian children come home for lunch at about 1:00. Sometimes they nap then, but they always leave time for studying before they relax with friends or their favorite pastimes. They do not go to school at all in the afternoon, so they can do homework until late afternoon and still have time to invite someone over.

In an alcove, Camille keeps her favorite stuffed animals.

Like many teenage girls in Brazil, Camille collects stationery. Shops sell it one sheet at a time, with matching envelopes and stickers called *fofuras*. Some stationery comes in a series. A series might have similar pictures or matching colors or designs. Girls trade stationery with one another so that they can fill out their series, much as some children trade baseball cards.

Camille is quite proud of her collection. She keeps it in a large drawer in her room. When guests come to her house, she likes to show it to them and explain what she has collected.

Camille's shelves, with books and special treasures.

"Let me show you my series with drawings of animals on it."

From her bedroom window, Camille can watch the treetops sway.

A Children's Party

Like all Brazilian children, Camille likes parties. Tonight she will be going to a birthday party, so it is especially important that she nap. The children bring gifts to one another, as guests usually do at birthday parties. But they also share in bringing the food and drinks.

Cariocas children also have discos in downtown Rio that are only for them. Parents drop them off and pick them up. Brazilians love to dance, so children are able to learn steps when they are young by going to the discos. Camille would rather party with her friends.

Tonight Camille joins many of her friends at Bobby's house. He is celebrating his 12th birthday. Bobby is one of Camille's best friends. He is in her grade, but he goes to a different school so they only see one another after school. They like to study together, go to movies, and listen to music.

Friends will come to Bobby's house at about 6:00 in the evening. While boys do not have many restrictions, girls have a curfew. Camille's father will come back for her at midnight. The children dance, snack on cookies, fruit, and fruit juice, and chatter with one another. When Bobby begins to get impatient, they let him open his presents.

"Does this shirt look all right?"

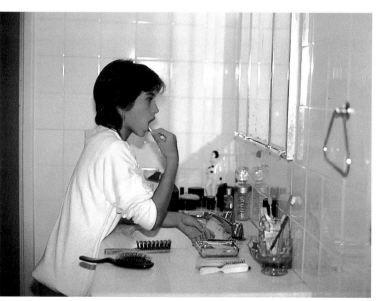

Camille brushes her teeth before the party.

Some of the children are shy about dancing.

Camille is the sixth one in from the right, under the lamp.

Students can arrange their desks as they like.

Social studies and English textbooks.

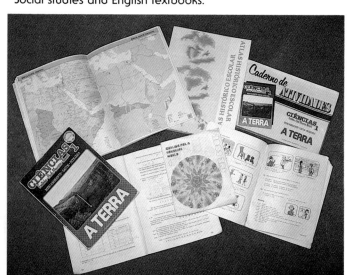

André's New School

In Brazil the summer months, when school is out, are January and February. The school year starts in early March.

André has been having trouble in school. He is supposed to be in 7th grade. But he is in 5th because he changed schools twice and dropped out for six months. So he fell behind his class. He hopes everything will be better this year. He likes his new school and is making friends.

"I'm getting pretty good at soccer."

Theater class meets outside today.

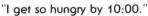

"I get so hungry by 10:00."

School starts at 7:30. Each of the five classes lasts 50 minutes. André takes Portuguese (the national language), math, social studies, English, physical education, and theater. Theater is his favorite class. Students buy snacks during the 10:00 break and still have time for some sports activity.

One of André's drawings.

After break, André has math and social studies. He has some problems today with math, but he answers many questions in social studies and is proud of himself. He believes that even though he is behind his class, he will catch up eventually.

André is in the second row, second from the left.

Camille's School

Camille's school is on Santa Teresa Hill. At one time, her school building was a beautiful foreign embassy. Even now it looks like a castle on the outside.

Camille's school is considered one of the more difficult schools in Rio, so the children must work very hard. Camille likes all of her courses, although her favorite is math. She is beginning to wonder if she can be a mathematician as well as an actress when she grows up!

Camille's drawing. Sometimes she and André like to compare their art work.

The bus in front of Camille's beautiful school building.

There are about 900 students from kindergarten through senior high school. The 6th grade has two classes, with a total of about 45 students. Many grade schools in Brazil are private. Students must pay tuition and buy their books. The public schools are free, so families with little money send their children there.

Talking during recess.

Camille likes to sit next to the teacher.

Camille is in class 6B. She is in the center.

Camille is a good athlete and particularly likes to play volleyball. Today in physical education, she plays basketball. She is disappointed when her team loses. She thinks it is because the opposing team has Roberto, the class's best player.

Camille goes after the ball.

Pão de Açucar (Sugar Loaf Mountain) rises above the white sand of Ipanema Beach.

Brazilians love to dance.

Weekend Trips to the Beach

In January and February, the hottest summer months, temperatures sometimes soar over 100°F (38°C). In northern Brazil, close to the equator, summer temperatures commonly hover above 90°F (32°C). With such heat, Brazilians love their beaches.

The family enjoys Ipanema, one of Rio's famous beaches. Another one well known to North Americans is Copacabana Beach. Lining the beach are large hotels and apartment buildings where tourists stay. Tourists and Cariocas alike must be careful, though. On the beaches are pickpockets, some of them children, who take wallets from blankets, purses, and pockets.

But visitors still enjoy the beach. Some play musical instruments. Others dance the samba. For refreshments, they drink coconut milk through a hole they make in the shell. Then they break the shell into smaller pieces and eat the white fruit inside. Brazil produces so much fruit that people drink fruit juices instead of soft drinks.

The family walks on Ipanema Beach. Marli and Camille wear the *tanga* ("string"), a tiny bikini that became popular worldwide after it appeared in Rio.

"Watch me, Camille!" says André.

Many Brazilians do not swim, despite living so close to the
ocean. They splash around in the water and enjoy the sand
and sun. Marli says Camille and André can swim better than
she does. But other sports take place along the shore.
People surf, wind-surf, and play volleyball and soccer on the
beach. All social classes and all ages enjoy the shore equally.
It is a place to see old friends and meet new ones.

André has a treasure he found on the beach when he was only
seven. It is an engraved amulet, a kind of charm people wear on a
chain around their necks. When he isn't wearing it, André keeps
his amulet safe in a drawer at home.

André treasures his amulet. ▶

Elías Manez-Silver's antique shop.

At the Markets

Elías Manez-Silver owns an antique shop filled with old, interesting objects. The family's living room is furnished with some of these antiques. It took Elías 20 years to collect pieces for his store. He has had to read books to find out when certain pieces were made and what they were made of. Knowing the history of an antique makes it more fun for the person who owns it. He goes to auctions and sales to find articles that he believes people would like.

André looks at glassware with his father.

André likes the antique toys.

André likes to go to the antique market with his father. Once he bought a plate with his own money and put it in his father's shop. When it was sold, the money went into André's savings account.

Today André plans to pick out something at the market all by himself, without his father's help. André likes computers and wants to study them when he grows up. But he also thinks an antique dealer's life would be interesting.

Camille asks her father to buy her a flower for her hair.

On Sunday the family goes to the open-air market, where vendors sell fruit, vegetables, and flowers all year round. Elías and Camille buy the groceries. They pick out bananas, pineapples, mangos, oranges, carrots, lettuce, and beans. The bananas, from the Amazon, are round and sweet. Brazil is rich in many kinds of bananas, so the price is cheap.

"Extra Delicious" oranges.

Camille has chosen what she wants.

"Look at all the herbs and spices."

André helps Marli select roses.

"I like almonds in my chocolate bars."

Marli prefers the flower shop and sweet shop, where she can buy different kinds of chocolate. André is learning about flowers, so he goes with her. Camille likes family shopping day because she knows Marli or Elías will usually buy her something.

Brazil's farm and grazing land adds up to the size of Quebec, or twice the size of Texas. From the ocean, Brazilians gather many kinds of seafood. Because the country does not need to import seafood, fruits, vegetables, meats, and poultry, food costs less than it does in countries with little farmland.

The children practice dancing the night before Carnival.

Camille and her friend Janaiya put on makeup.

André shows off his costume.

Catching a ride on the streetcar.

Dancing around the streetcar.

Carnival

In late February, just before Lent, everyone in Brazil celebrates *Carnaval* (Carnival). For four days and five nights, people fill the streets. They eat and drink and dance to samba music.

The streetcars get crowded at Carnival time.

Carnival ends on Ash Wednesday. Brazilians spend lots of money on costumes, even the poorest people. Everyone plans costumes, dances, and skits months ahead of time.

Up Santa Teresa Hill comes the streetcar, decorated for Carnival. It is filled with many people throwing confetti. Camille and André join a dancing parade. They climb up the hill, doing the samba around the streetcar. This streetcar is 90 years old, and the people who live on Santa Teresa love it very much. Some people want to take if off the street, but others like its old-fashioned charm.

37

Dancers do not mind being caught in a rainstorm.

People from around the world visit Rio during Carnival. Shantytown neighborhoods (*favelas*) organize into groups called samba "schools." They practice their songs, skits, and dances so they can win a prize. There might be 3,000 dancers and musicians in one school. During Carnival, judges vote on the dancing, floats, costumes, and music. The best schools parade before Cariocas and tourists alike. People come from all over Brazil and the world to see this yearly celebration.

"Do you think our costumes will win first prize?"

A parade with a helium-filled clown.

"If we're going to dance for four days, let's wear more comfortable shoes!"

Businesses and stores close for the four days of Carnival. Only the street vendors continue to work. They sell food and drink to those who need refreshments after the dancing and parading. The streets are filled with trash left by all the people. But by noon on Ash Wednesday, the streets are clean again. Then begins the quiet period of Lent.

Some parts of town do not invite others to celebrate Carnival on their street. Other areas charge admission. Tonight the family decides to go to Rio Branco because that neighborhood does want guests and charges no admission.

Brazilians are fun-loving people. Music, dance, sports, and other forms of relaxation are important to them. While other countries have fine carnivals before Lent, no carnival seems as lively as Brazil's.

Camille and André wear costumes but their parents do not.

Food stalls usually sell corn, sausages, and different kinds of drinks.

They are caught in rain on the way to Rio Branco. But this does not surprise or disappoint them. February is a summer month in Brazil, and summer is the rainy season. So people are used to being rained on. They keep dancing. Some crowd around the food stalls. Soon the rain will let up; the warm air will dry everyone's clothes; and the people will continue enjoying themselves.

Camille and André want to go to the parade so they can see the winning samba schools. This parade goes on quite late, however, and Marli and Elías are not sure the children should stay up.

Corcovado Hill

People can take streetcars or cable cars to Corcovado Hill.

One nice day, the family goes to Corcovado Hill. On it stands the statue of Christ the Redeemer, built in the 1920s to celebrate the 100th anniversary of Brazilian independence from Portugal. The statue is nearly 120 feet high (36 m). Its arms are about 92 feet (28 m) from fingertip to fingertip. It weighs 700 tons. Inside the statue is a small chapel.

Having a snack on the lookout platform.

Behind Camille and André is the
huge statue, Christ the Redeemer.

At night, lights illuminate the statue of Christ.

In the evening, from
Corcovado Hill, Rio looks
like a string of diamonds
circling the inlets of the
Atlantic. People who have
visited Rio believe that it is
one of the most beautiful
cities in the world. Marli and
Elías and Camille and André
would agree.

Sparkling Rio seen from Corcovado Hill.

FOR YOUR INFORMATION: Brazil

Official name: República Federativa do Brasil
(Hey-PU-blee-kah Feh-deh-rah-CHEE-vah dew Brah-ZEEO)
The Federative Republic of Brazil

Capital: Brasília

History

Brazil is a vast country. It has both large modern cities and areas of swamp, grassland, and dense jungle that few people have seen. The land has not been easy to settle because of its size, its weather, and its jungle. Brazilians in remote areas know little about Brazilians in other states. Many people cannot read or write. The Brazilian people are still struggling to provide food, housing, and education for everyone. In many ways, Brazil straddles the past and the present.

Brazil's Native Inhabitants

Scattered tribes of American Indians first lived in the area we call Brazil. Some, like the Guaicuru, roamed across the land. They were excellent at raising, training, and riding

The beautiful City Theater in Rio, the capital of Brazil from 1763 until 1960.

horses. Their descendants, the Kadiweu, are still brilliant horsemen. Other tribes, like the Guaná, were farmers and remained somewhat settled. In the 15th century, Spain and Portugal competed in settling new lands in the Americas. Spain landed in North America in 1492. Eight years later, in 1500, Admiral Pedro Alvares Cabral led the Portuguese to northeastern South America. Their first important settlement, Salvador, was the capital of Brazil until 1763.

Portuguese Colonialism and Slavery

To make a living, these early settlers cut and sold Brazil-wood. Later they developed sugar cane plantations. To work the fields, settlers brought another group of people to Brazil — African slaves. They came against their will. Landowners had tried using Indians for fieldwork. But knowing the land, Indians would escape into the woods. For the next 150 years, the Portuguese, Africans, and Indians intermarried, and settlements grew. The Portuguese fought Spanish, Dutch, and English expeditions that also came to settle this vast land.

More European Interest

In the late 16th century, miners found precious gems to the south and west of Salvador. In Europe, news of jewels that could be scooped from the ground brought the Dutch, French, Italians, and Germans to Brazil. Seaports such as Rio de Janeiro grew, and in the 17th century, people made wealthy by the mines began to build cities and develop cultural interests.

Independence from Portugal

By the late 18th century, Brazil no longer wanted to be a colony of Portugal. In 1808, when Napoleon invaded Lisbon and took control of Portugal, Prince John of Portugal and his family escaped to Brazil. In 1822, Brazil made his son, Dom Pedro, its emperor. Brazilians stopped importing slaves in 1853, abolished slavery in 1888, and decided they no longer wanted an emperor in 1889. They wrote a constitution based on the US constitution. At about this time, large numbers of Europeans and Japanese were migrating to Brazil.

Modern Brazil: What Type of Democracy?

In 1930, a military government overthrew the president, and a dictator governed until 1945. From 1945 to 1961, presidents governed. But economic unrest worried the military, and they again took control in 1961. In 1985 they gave up power, hoping to let the people elect the president. Right now, Brazil has limited elections. Congress and representatives from each state are the ones who elect the president, not the people.

The People — Population and Ethnic Groups

In 1985, the population of Brazil was 135,000,000. Brazilians are primarily of European, American Indian, and African origin. Unlike North Americans, Brazilians do not indicate precise racial differences for census purposes. Anyone light-skinned is considered white, anyone darker-skinned with signs of European ancestry is mulatto or mestizo, and anyone with obvious Negroid features is black. Whites make up about 60% of the population; mulattos and mestizos about 25%, blacks about 8%; Orientals and Indians, the remainder.

About 220,000 Indians remain in Brazil. This number grows each year in some areas because of nutrition and medical care. But other tribes suffer from both the white man's diseases and the railroads and highways being built in their areas. Today many Indians live on reservations. Once they were able to live off these lands. But by the 1960s they had begun to buy and sell goods in nearby towns. Now many Indians living on reservations work on ranches or in cities.

Brazil has a serious population problem. The country is huge, so there is room for many people. But 90% of them live along the Atlantic Ocean. Life is very hard for these people right now. A great gap exists between the rich and poor. Many children are not being taken care of. As of 1987, 550,000 children lived in government homes; 7 million had few ties to their families and were beggars or pickpockets in the larger cities; and 36 million were classified as "needy." Both children and adults need work. Since the 1960s, many farms and rural businesses have failed, so people have moved to the overcrowded cities seeking jobs. Those who do find work barely make enough to live on. But most have no jobs, so the government hopes to settle them on farms and ranches in the *sertão*, the interior of Brazil.

Language

English is taught in the schools; the national language is Portuguese. Indian and immigrant languages, particularly French, have changed pronunciation and usage. So Brazilian Portuguese does not sound like Portuguese in Portugal. Indians speak their own languages as well as Portuguese. People are recording these Indian languages before civilization causes them to vanish.

Education

About 90% of the grade schools are public; most high schools are run by the Roman Catholic Church. Public schools are free, but students pay for private schools and buy their books as well. Because so many people in Brazil are poor, they cannot afford school. Half of the children who do go to school do not pass first grade because they have to drop out to work or are too hungry to study. Many do not go back to repeat the grade. Students who make it to high school and can afford to go attend for three years.

Over 57 public and private universities are available for those who want to attend college. Students who attend must first pass the *Vestibular*, a very difficult exam. Some students study an entire year before taking the exam. And even then many must take the exam more than once before they pass it.

Over 750 other schools provide special kinds of training. The country needs scientists, plumbers, electricians, and computer programmers, so some schools teach these practical courses. Trade schools graduate more students than universities do. A public system, using volunteer teachers, helps teach adults to read. The Armed Forces teach reading, writing, and job skills to military people. Businesses are also teaching reading because they have found that people who cannot read signs cause damage to themselves and equipment. To reach the people in the Amazon, volunteers from colleges and universities are spending summers teaching in the Amazon Rain Forest. Courses taught by radio also reach Brazilians in remote areas.

Religion

About 90% of the population is Catholic. In the northeast, many hold African spiritualist beliefs. A Jewish population is centered in the larger cities. Other Brazilians have Protestant or Indian beliefs. Brazilians consider themselves religious people, but most do not go to church except on special occasions.

Government

Brazil has had a constitution since the 19th century, but it has also had military rulers for many years. Most leaders have stressed social reform and economic growth, but some have imprisoned or tortured people who disagreed with them.

Like the US, Brazil has three branches of government: executive, legislative, and judicial. The president serves one term of six years. The legislature is made up of two groups: the 72-member Senate (three from each of Brazil's 23 states, and one federal district), and the Chamber of Deputies, whose size varies. Senators serve eight-year terms and deputies four-year terms. The judicial branch is made up of 11 judges chosen by the president and approved by the Senate.

Brazil's politics reflect the problems of its economy. The country has serious troubles with inflation. This means that its money keeps losing value. For example, one day a popsicle might cost a Brazilian child 5 cents, the next day 10 cents, the next day 15 cents, and so on. It other words, the cost of the popsicle keeps inflating, or getting higher. Government leaders try to stop inflation by freezing prices. They won't let merchants charge more. Or leaders change the value of money so one day a dollar may be worth 10 cents. All of this makes people angry. When they can't be certain how much their money is worth, they want new governments.

Currency

Brazil's monetary unit is the New Cruzado. Bills have been in denominations of 1, 5, 10, 50, 100, 200, 500, 1,000, and 5,000. But recently the treasury has begun replacing bills below 100 with coins of equal value. Because of serious inflation in Brazil, it is uncertain how much a cruzado is worth in Canadian and US dollars.

Land

Overall Land Area

Brazil is on the northeastern side of South America. It has an area of 3,290,000 sq miles (8,521,100 sq km). It is slightly larger than the continental United States, and it borders every South American country except Chile and Ecuador. Its Atlantic eastern coast has about 4,600 miles (7,401 km) of shoreline. If we straightened out all the coves and peninsulas along the shore, this would equal the distance between Toronto and Moscow. Convenient harbors and huge river systems make sea trade easy for Brazil.

The Five Regions of Brazil

Because of Brazil's vast size, people differ regionally much as they do in regions of the US or Canada. Here is a look at Brazil's five geographic sections.

The North — This is the Brazil we see in the movies. It holds the Amazon River and the dense Amazon Rain Forest. The 80°F (27°C) temperatures are uncomfortable because of the humidity. The annual rainfall is 87 inches (221 cm), about double the rainfall of St. Louis or Montreal. In this area is Manaus, a city made duty-free in 1967 to attract assembly plants to the area. Businesses do not pay taxes on their goods, and shoppers can buy everything cheaply. Oceangoing vessels from the Atlantic ship goods up and down the rivers. So far only about 6,000,000 people live in this huge section of Brazil, fewer people than in metropolitan Chicago.

The Northeast — Temperatures here hover in the 90s and 100s F (32-38°C). The average rainfall is 49 inches (125 cm). This seems like a lot of rain, but this area experiences drought much of the time. Then when it rains, it pours. It was to this area that ships brought African slaves. About 26% of all Brazilians live in the northeast.

West Central — In this area are the Federal District of Brasília and the Pantanal region. The Pantanal, the size of South Dakota, is a wild marshland of rivers and clear lakes. It is one of the last virgin forests in the world. Brasília, the capital of Brazil since 1960, is in the southeastern corner of this area.

The Southeast — About 53,000,000, or nearly 40%, of Brazil's people live here, partly because this is an important port of entry to Brazil. Two major cities here are Rio de Janeiro and São Paulo. Rio is an art, fashion, and jewelry center. It also has famous beaches like Ipanema and Copacabana. Rio was the capital for years, and as such it became an important cultural center. Today, Rio is filled with museums and libraries. But Rio is also known for its *favelas*, shantytowns for the poor. While many Brazilian cities have favelas, Rio's are probably the worst. With no running water, children carry cooking water from nearby wells

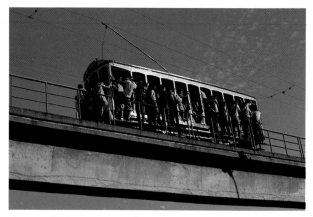
A crowded streetcar in Rio.

and rivers. People wash their clothes in rivers. Human waste runs down the streets, carried by rains into the nearest sewers and rivers. Disease is widespread. São Paulo, slightly south and inland, attracts people in business and industry. It is one of the fastest growing cities in the world. Rich soil in the state of São Paulo provides half Brazil's coffee, cotton, fruit, and vegetables. The area offers up to 500,000 new jobs each year, helping to fight Brazil's poverty problems.

The Southern Region — Nearly 20,000,000 people live in the south. It is a land of flat plains and forested mountains that sometimes get snow. Germans and Italians living here developed ranches and plantations. They also put up buildings reminding them of Europe. The Gaúcho Cultural Center in the city of Porto Alegre honors the cowboys (Gaúchos) who worked on the flat pampas grasslands of this region. This is still Gaúcho country. Where the Paraná and the Paranapanéma Rivers meet is Iguaçú Falls, the largest falls in the world. Its waters send up rainbow clouds of mist and cause the surrounding countryside to tremble.

The Amazon Basin

The Amazon Basin is made up of the Amazon River and Rain Forest. The Amazon River, at 3,900 miles (6,275 km), is second only to the Nile in length. It is so wide that oceangoing vessels can travel on it. It runs through the hot, humid, and dense Amazon Forest that takes up 40% of Brazil's land.

Hundreds of species of plants grow everywhere. These include some poisonous plants that contain the deadly *curare* used by Amazon Indians for arrowheads. Countless species of insects, birds, and mammals thrive in the forest. The river holds the 15-foot-long *pirarucú* (Amazon redfish), the longest fish in the world, as well as the deadly flesh-eating fish, the *piranha*.

The Amazon Basin is in trouble. Settlers, cattle barons, miners, and hunters hack into the trees to find land for coffee, cacão, sugar cane, and cattle. Construction crews carve out chunks of forest for a transcontinental highway. Amazon Forest Indians are in danger of losing their way of life, and animal and plant species will be destroyed. Environmentalists everywhere worry because they believe 50% of the earth's oxygen comes from this forest. But Brazil's leaders want people to clear the forest and move out of overcrowded cities. They believe Brazil's economy will grow if a highway crosses the South American continent and makes shipping easier.

Climate

Brazil's seasons are just the reverse of those in North America. Summer, when temperatures can go up to 120°F (49°C), is from December through March. During the winter, temperatures get as low as 50°F (10°C) in some areas. Brazil's size results in five different climate types: the equatorial Amazon (warm and humid), the semi-arid northeast (warm and dry), the tropical central region (warm with a dry season), the altitude tropical southeast (mild all year), and the subtropical south (warm summers and cool winters).

Brazil's climate provides year-round flowers.

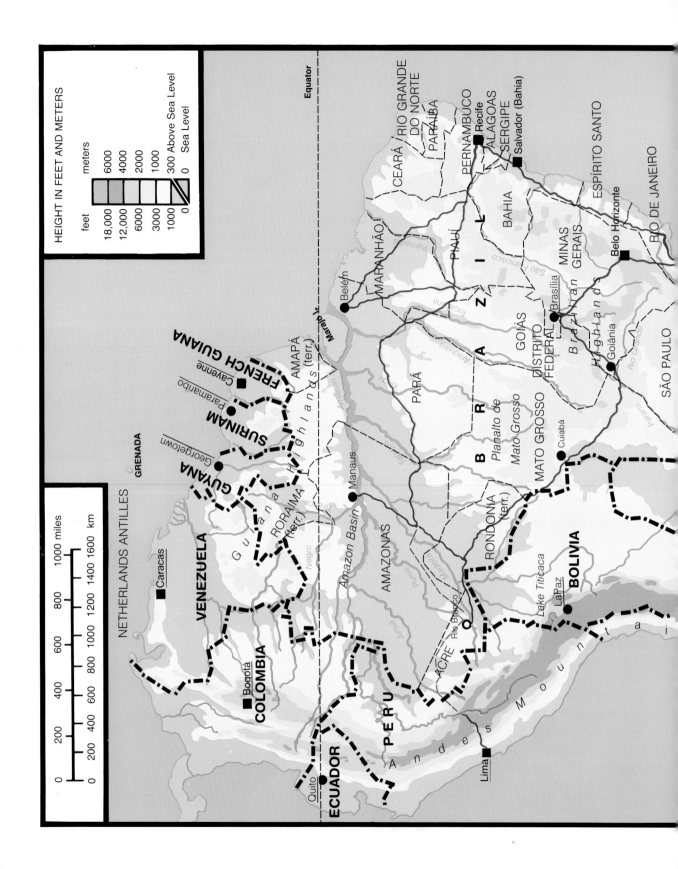

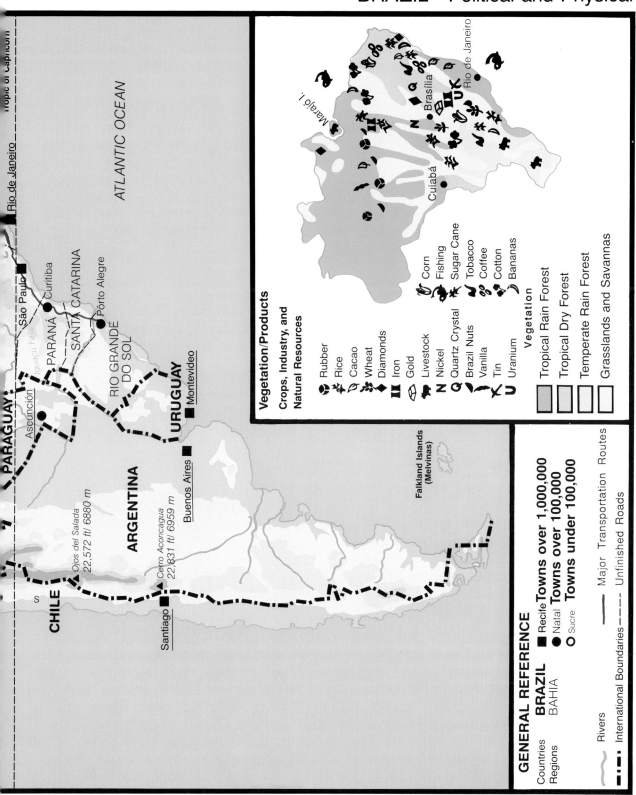

ATLANTIC OCEAN

Rio de Janeiro

Tropic of Capricorn

São Paulo
Curitiba
SANTA CATARINA
PARANA
Porto Alegre
RIO GRANDE DO SUL
Iguaçu Falls
Asunción
PARAGUAY
Montevideo
URUGUAY
Buenos Aires
ARGENTINA
Ojos del Salada 22,572 ft/ 6880 m
Cerro Aconcagua 22,831 ft/ 6959 m
CHILE
S
Santiago
Falkland Islands (Melvinas)

Vegetation/Products

Crops, Industry, and Natural Resources

- Rubber
- Rice
- Cacao
- Wheat
- Diamonds
- Iron
- Gold
- Livestock
- Nickel
- Quartz Crystal
- Brazil Nuts
- Vanilla
- Tin
- Uranium

- Corn
- Fishing
- Sugar Cane
- Tobacco
- Coffee
- Cotton
- Bananas

Marajó I.
Brasília
Rio de Janeiro
Cuiabá

Vegetation

- Tropical Rain Forest
- Tropical Dry Forest
- Temperate Rain Forest
- Grasslands and Savannas

GENERAL REFERENCE

Countries	**BRAZIL**
Regions	BAHIA

- ■ Recife **Towns over 1,000,000**
- ● Natal **Towns over 100,000**
- ○ Sucre **Towns under 100,000**

—— Major Transportation Routes

–––– Unfinished Roads

∿ Rivers

■-·-■ International Boundaries

Natural Resources

Brazil is rich in minerals. It mines bauxite, copper, nickel, gold, silver, lead, mica, titanium, manganese, uranium, coal, asbestos, tin, and industrial diamonds. It provides 13% of the world's total iron ore. It also exports natural gas and crude petroleum.

Industry

Brazil is the largest industrial country in South America. It employs over 25% of its people in industry. It is the second largest producer of iron ore in the world, the fourth largest producer of wood and radios, and the tenth largest of motor vehicles. Brazilians also produce textiles, chemicals, cement, heavy machinery, and steel products. Look at the labels on some of your shoes; many shoes sold in North America are being made in Brazil. Rich soil means Brazilians do not need to import food, but industry must import some machinery, chemicals, and cereals. Brazil's major trading partners are the US, West Germany, the Netherlands, and Japan.

Agriculture

Historically, Brazil has always focused on one major crop at a time. These crops have been Brazil-wood, sugar, coffee, and rubber. Brazilians farm and graze about 20% of the land. This comes out to 658,000 sq miles (1,704,220 sq km), a land area twice the size of Texas and about the size of Quebec. Agriculture employs 30-35% of the population. The country is the world's second largest supplier of coffee and sugar and the third largest supplier of corn, soybeans, and livestock such as beef cattle, dairy cattle, and pigs. Brazil also harvests seafood off the long Atlantic coastline. Other products raised in Brazil are tobacco, cotton, rice, beans, oranges, nuts, and bananas.

Art and Culture

Architecture

Brazil's younger cities often focus on industrial growth. But older cities are best known for their art and architecture. In 1941, the government created a group that encourages Brazilians to preserve the art and architecture of their region. The people of one older city, Salvador, Brazil's capital until 1763, have certainly done so. Its streets are lined with hand-chipped bricks, just as they were in the 17th century, and 20,000 of the city's 97,000 buildings are over 250 years old.

Gold and precious gems were discovered in Brazil in the late 16th century. Wealthy miners brought skilled workers such as sculptors, stonemasons, and carpenters from Europe to build impressive churches and palaces. Most of these structures remain. Some are now museums, but many of the churches continue to hold services. One famous sculptor was a mulatto Brazilian named Antonio Francisco Lisboa (known as "Aleijadinho"). He created wood and stone carvings for many churches in Ouro Prêto ("Black Gold"). This city is important historically to Brazilians because rebellion against the Portuguese began there. When Aleijadinho became crippled from leprosy, his assistants tied his hammer and chisel to his wrists so that he could continue his work. Tourists visit these treasures today, just as they do the famous cathedrals of Europe.

The entire wall of this building in Rio is a painting.

Painting

Today, Brazilian artists create works that reflect the national personality. The Dutch brought European ideas about painting to Brazil in the 18th century, and they taught Brazilian painters such as Manuel da Cunha. A former slave, da Cunha was sent by his master to Lisbon to study portrait painting. In 1816, a burst of artistic energy resulted when members of the French Art Mission came to Brazil. Two Brazilians taught by them, Pedro Américo (1843-1905) and Victor Meireles (1832-1903), painted huge scenes about Brazil's history. In the 20th century, another cultural event, Modern Art Week, brought international artists and new life to Brazil's art community. Brazil began earning a reputation for its impressionists, engravers, and book illustrators. A famous modern painter, Cândido Portineri (1903-1962), chose common people for his subjects. His murals about war and peace are in the United Nations Building in New York City.

Literature

Brazilians produce half the books in Portuguese published in Latin America. The history of Brazil's literature reflects its development as a country. Poets in the Colonial Period (1500-1822) helped inspire the rebellion against the Portuguese. In the Romantic Period (1822-1879), poets explored folklore and African and American Indian themes. In the post-Romantic period (1879-1922) poets focused on precision in rhythm and words, and novelists began writing realistic fiction that startled some readers. The Modern Period (1922-present) has brought experimenting to poetry. Modern novelists write about regions of Brazil, history, and the lives of average people.

Music

Early music in Brazil was influenced by religion and European traditions. In 1889, after Brazilians broke ties to Portugal, composers emphasized Brazilian themes. Modern Art Week in 1922 brought great life to music. One world-famous composer attending that gathering was Heitor Villa-Lobos (1887-1959). He used rhythms and melodies from folklore in many of his 1700 compositions. Popular music has many forms. The most well-known in North America are the samba and a sophisticated form of the samba known as *bossa nova*.

Soccer, the national passion.

Sports and Entertainment

Sports

Spectator Sports — Like North Americans, Brazilians enjoy many spectator sports such as basketball, volleyball, tennis, boxing, and auto racing. Brazil has won the World Basketball Championship once, and Maria Ester Bueno from São Paulo won the singles title twice at both Wimbledon and Forest Hills. Eder Jofre was world champion twice in boxing. In 1972 and 1974, Emerson Fittipaldi won the world championship in auto racing. But soccer *(futebol)* fills Brazil's huge stadiums. The world has long admired Brazil's talented player, Pêlé (Edson Arantes do Nascimento). Led by Pêlé, Brazil won the World Cup in 1958, 1962, and 1970. While soccer fans in some countries get nasty, Brazilian fans are good-natured.

Recreational Sports — Brazilians also love to play sports. They join clubs or societies to go mountain climbing, water-skiing, underwater diving, and spelunking (cave exploring). Recently the government has decided to build sports complexes throughout Brazil. About 90% of Brazilians live along the coast, so many of their activities take place on or near beaches. They surf, wind-surf, ride bicycles, and play soccer and volleyball along the shore. The well-to-do enjoy yachting and fishing off their yachts in ocean waters.

Capueira — This sport is a mix of fighting, dancing, and judo. It developed because slavemasters would punish slaves caught fighting. So men who wished to fight would mask their activity through dance-like combat that eventually became *capueira*. The sport is practiced primarily by black males in Recife and Salvador. It requires great agility and dexterity. Players thrust at one another using only their legs, feet, heels, and heads.

Entertainment

Dance — Brazilians love music and dance. The popular samba music has its roots in Africa. In cities, dancers go to discos and *gafieira* halls in which they show off their skills.

Ethnic Traditions — In Brazil, different ethnic traditions dominate in each region. When settlers first came to these regions, they used what nature offered in each area and adapted it to traditions from their homelands. For example, in Bahía, traditions brought by Africans appear in music, instruments, spiritualism, myths, and legends. Foods that have become traditional in this area are *vatapá*, a dish based on the shrimp and fish that are found in the area; *sarapatel*, a stew made from the liver or heart of sheep or pigs; and *carurú*, another stew of shrimp, okra, onions, and red peppers.

Gaúchos (cowboys) who live in Rio Grande do Sul like *churrasco* (barbecue). They put chunks of beef on a sword, broil the beef, stick the sword into a wooden tabletop, and carve off the pieces they want. They also drink máte tea from a gourd; this tea, called *chimarrão*, is made from dried evergreen leaves. The Germans who have settled in the São Paulo region have brought their beer-making skills from Europe with them, and the Italians have carried on the practice of making wine. Today, descendants of the original Italians are producing excellent wines and shipping them to France and Italy. In France these wines are mixed with French wines and sold as "authentic" French wines.

Carnival — The national period of merrymaking, Carnival *(Carnaval)*, begins at 11:00 p.m. on the Friday before Ash Wednesday, the day Lent begins. This grand celebration lasts four days and five nights. Rio's Carnival is world-famous. People travel from all over the world to take part. Brazil's social classes celebrate Carnival in different ways. The poor from each neighborhood organize samba "schools" that can consist of as many as 3,000 people. Some dance; some act in skits; others play in the *bateria*, a marching band with drums and percussion instruments. For a year before Carnival, these groups plan costumes, floats, skits, dancing, and music. At Carnival, they compete with other schools. The twelve winners parade for spectators. All, of course, want the top prize. Middle-class Brazilians may watch samba schools in the streets, but they also celebrate Carnival with parties at friends' homes. The upper class attends costume balls in lavish dress based on legend and fairy tales.

Brasília

In the 1950s, the government decided to move the capital from Rio to dry, dusty Brasília. It hired two architects to design the city. Lúcio Costa was to lay out the city. Oscar Niemeyer, architect of the United Nations building in New York City, was to plan the buildings. Neimeyer's buildings are among the world's most beautiful examples of modern architecture. Costa designed the city in the shape of an airplane, with the "wings" to be used for businesses and homes. In the "nose" are hotels and commercial buildings. In the center are government buildings housing the ministry. And in the "tail" are the Senate, the Chamber of Deputies, the Palace of Justice, and the President's Palace. Residential areas are laid out in *Super Quadro* ("Super Blocks"). In each block are a chapel, a primary school, a shopping center, and both luxury and low-cost apartments.

Brazilians in North America

Many thousands of Brazilians visit North America each year. Some come to represent their businesses or the government, but the vast majority come to vacation. Around 190,000 visited the US alone in 1985; of these, about 140,000 were vacationing. That same year, about 13,500 visited Canada. Few Brazilians move north permanently. In the last ten years, only 1,500-2,500 per year have become citizens of the US, and only 160-330 of Canada. The majority of those who do come to North America for work, pleasure, or permanent residency enter through large cities like Miami and New York in the US and Toronto and Vancouver in Canada. Many remain in the large cities where they enter. Here, they live near other Brazilians, while others join family members in other places who may have preceded them north.

More Books About Brazil

Here are some books about Brazil. If you are interested in them, check your library. Some may be helpful in doing research for the "Things to Do" projects that follow.

Born to Dance Samba. Cohen (Harper and Row)
Brazil. Cross (Childrens Press)
Brazil in Pictures. (Lerner)
Looking at Brazil. Kendall (Lippincott)
Take a Trip to Brazil. Lye (Franklin Watts)
Tales from the Amazon. Elbl (Penworthy)
We Live in Brazil. Robb (Franklin Watts)

Glossary of Useful Brazilian Terms

bateria (ba-tah-REE-ah)	a marching band of drums and cymbals; part of a samba school during Carnival
bossa nova (boh-sah NO-vah)	a more complex form of the samba
capueira (kah-pu-WA-rah)	a difficult sport resembling a mix of dance and judo; played by black males in Recife and Salvador
Cariocas (kar-ee-O-kas)	residents of Rio
Carnaval (kah-nah-VAH-u)	the world-famous celebration held before Lent
carurú (kah-ru-RU)	a stew of shrimp, okra, onions, and red peppers; tradition of northeast
chimarrão (shee-mah-HOW)	tea drunk by Gaúchos; made from dried leaves of evergreen trees; máte tea
churrasco (shu-HAS-ko)	a Gaúcho barbecue
Corcovado Hill (koh-koh-VAH-do)	hill from which you can see Rio
curare (ku-rah-RA)	poison Amazon Indians extract from plants and use on arrows
Dona (DO-nah)	term used before the first name of an older woman to show respect
favelas (fah-VEL-us)	slums in Rio

feijão (fa-JAH-o)	a bean dish
fofuras (fo-FU-ras)	stickers girls buy to match pieces of stationery in their collections
futebol (FU-chee-ball)	Brazilian term for soccer
gafieria (gah-fee-YA-rah)	dance halls in the cities
Gamafillo (gah-mah-FEE-yo)	university Marli and Elías attended
Gaúchos (gow-U-shos)	Brazilian cowboys
Iguaçú Falls (ee-gwa-SU)	largest waterfall in the world, located in Brazil
manjioca (man-JO-kah)	a kind of potato
Pão de Açucar (pow da a-SU-kar) . .	Sugar Loaf Mountain in Rio
piranha (pee-RAH-nyah)	deadly flesh-eating Amazon fish
pirarucú (pee-rah-ru-KU)	Amazon fish 15 feet (5 m) long
São Paulo (sow POW-lo)	large city in Brazil
sarapatel (sah-ra-pa-TEW)	a dish made from the liver or heart of sheep or pigs; tradition of northeast
senhor (seen-YOR)	term used to show respect to men
sertão (sir-TAH-o)	the interior of Brazil
vatapá (va-TAH-pah)	a dish using shrimp and fish; tradition of northeast

Things to Do — Research Projects

The vast Amazon Basin is vital to the survival of the earth because it provides great quantities of oxygen humans need. For years, miners, farmers, and hunters have been cutting into the forest to use it for their purposes. Brazilians have been arguing about building a highway through this forest. They are concerned about damaging the balance of nature so badly that the world will suffer. As you read about Brazil in general or what is happening to the Amazon Basin in particular, keep in mind the importance of current facts. Some of the research projects that follow need accurate, up-to-date information from current sources. Two publications your library may have will tell you about recent newspaper and magazine articles on many topics:

Readers' Guide to Periodical Literature
Children's Magazine Guide

For accurate answers to questions about such topics of current interest as Brazil's work on the Amazon Basin, look up *Brazil* or the related topic in these two publications. They will lead you to the most up-to-date information you can find.

1. Two Brazilians are world-famous figures; one is the composer Heitor Villa-Lobos and the other is the soccer player Pêlé (Edson Arantes do Nascimento). Check the *Readers' Guide to Periodical Literature* or the *Children's Magazine Guide* for articles written about these men. Hint: go back to 1975 for Pêlé because he retired in 1974, and go back to 1960 for Villa-Lobos because he died in 1959.

2. Find out more about Brasília, the capital of Brazil. Why was it built? What is unusual about its design? What would be special for a child living in a city with that design?

3. The Carnival held in Rio each February is world-famous. Find out more about how it is celebrated.

4. What happens to the poor child in Brazil? Hundreds of thousands of children have no ties to their parents. What is life like for orphans such as these?

5. The government of Brazil has been shaky for years, although Brazilians are not the sort of people who are likely to have a violent revolution. The problem is related to inflation. Find out about the relationship between Brazil's inflation and its government.

More Things to Do — Activities

These projects are designed to encourage you to think more about Brazil. They offer interesting group or individual projects you can do at home or at school.

1. Brazil is divided into five regions with distinctly different geographical features. Using maps, atlases, travel guides, encyclopedias, and geography books, find out how the areas of the country differ. Draw a map of Brazil and fill in the areas of the country, showing jungle, flatlands, mountains, and major rivers.

2. If you would like a pen pal in Brazil, write to these people:

> International Pen Friends
> P.O. Box 290065
> Brooklyn, New York 11229-0001

Be sure to tell them what country you want your pen pal to be from. Also, include your full name, address, and age.

3. Brazilian cowboys, called *Gaúchos*, are still an important part of cattle raising. Read some books or encyclopedia articles about Gaúchos and about cowboys who worked in the North American west during the last part of the 19th century. Write an imaginary letter to a Gaúcho telling how his life differs from the life of the North American cowboy.

4. The enslavement of Africans by North and South Americans has been a shameful event in the histories of both continents. Find out more about the slave trade. How did it start? Who did it? How many Africans were captured and taken to the Americas? What were the ships like? What was slave life like in the Americas? How was life different for North American slaves than it was for South American slaves?

Index